TV COOKS

Valentina Harris

COOKS

Italian

Photographs by Philip Webb

Published by BBC Books,
an imprint of BBC Worldwide Publishing.
BBC Worldwide Limited, Woodlands,
80 Wood Lane, London W12 0TT.

The recipes in this book first appeared in the following:
Valentina Harris' Complete Italian Cookery Course
©Valentina Harris 1992
Valentina's Italian Regional Cookery
©Valentina Harris 1990

This edition first published 1996
©Valentina Harris 1996
The moral right of the author has been asserted

ISBN 0 563 38796 3

Edited by Pam Mallender
Designed by DW Design
Photographs by Philip Webb
Styling by Helen Payne
Home Economist Caroline Liddle

Set in New Caledonia and Helvetica
Printed and bound in Belgium by Proost NV
Colour separations by Colour Origination Ltd, London
Cover printed in Belgium by Proost NV

Cover and frontispiece: Roasted Peppers.

Contents

RECIPE NOTES

Eggs are size 2.
Wash all fresh produce before preparation and peel as necessary.
Spoon measurements are level. Always use proper measuring spoons:
1 teaspoon = 5ml and 1 tablespoon = 15ml.
Never mix metric or imperial measures in one recipe. Stick to one or the other.
Adjust seasoning or strongly flavoured ingredients to taste
If you substitute dried for fresh herbs, use half the amount.

HANDY CONVERSION TABLES

Weight		Volume		Linear	
15g	½oz	30ml	1fl oz	5mm	¼in
25g	1oz	50ml	2fl oz	10mm/1cm	½in
40g	1½oz	100ml	3½fl oz	2cm	¾in
55g	2oz	125ml	4fl oz	2.5cm	1in
85g	3oz	150ml	5fl oz (¼ pint)	5cm	2in
115g	4oz	175ml	6fl oz	7.5cm	3in
140g	5oz	200ml	7fl oz (⅓ pint)	10cm	4in
175g	6oz	225ml	8fl oz	13cm	5in
200g	7oz	250ml	9fl oz	15cm	6in
225g	8oz	300ml	10fl oz (½ pint)	18cm	7in
250g	9oz	350ml	12fl oz	20cm	8in
280g	10oz	400ml	14fl oz	23cm	9in
350g	12oz	425ml	15fl oz (¾ pint)	25cm	10in
375g	13oz	450ml	16fl oz	28cm	11in
400g	14oz	500ml	18fl oz	30cm	12in
425g	15oz	600ml	20fl oz (1 pint)		
450g	1lb	700ml	1¼ pints		
550g	1¼lb	850ml	1½ pints		
750g	1lb 10oz	1 litre	1¾ pints		
900g	2lb	1.2 litres	2 pints		
1kg	2¼lb	1.3 litres	2¼ pints		
1.3kg	3lb	1.4 litres	2½ pints		
1.8kg	4lb	1.7 litres	3 pints		
2.25kg	5lb	2 litres	3½ pints		
		2.5 litres	4½ pints		

Oven temperatures

225F	110C	GAS ¼
250F	120C	GAS ½
275F	140C	GAS 1
300F	150C	GAS 2
325F	160C	GAS 3
350F	180C	GAS 4
375F	190C	GAS 5
400F	200C	GAS 6
425F	220C	GAS 7
450F	230C	GAS 8
475F	240C	GAS 9

Ⓥ　Suitable for vegetarians

❇　Suitable for freezing

Italian food is my passion. The more I research and study, the more I discover. I sometimes think that I shall never really find all the recipes and ingredients which make up the gastronomy of this glorious country. In this collection, I have brought together some of my very favourite recipes. These are dishes which I continue to prepare at home for my family and friends, and which reflect just how versatile and wide ranging the cuisine of Italy can be. There is a lot more to whet your appetite in these pages than pizza or spaghetti bolognese!

Most Italian specialities are easy to prepare using ingredients which are now widely available. When I first came to live in England in the seventies I had enormous difficulty in fighting off the homesickness I felt for my native country, a homesickness which could only be cured by recreating the dishes I grew up with, because the ingredients seemed almost impossible to find. Nowadays, products such as good olive oil, fresh Parmesan, ricotta and mascarpone, Italian coffee and more are conveniently available almost anywhere. These days, when I go home to Italy I can go shopping for clothes and shoes to fill my suitcase rather than for vital food items!

I really hope you will enjoy these recipes and that you'll come back to them again and again, maybe adding a little something of your own from time to time if you feel the urge! I wish you *Buon Appetito*, with all my heart, and remember that food must above all be fun!

Valentina
xo

INGREDIENTS

Cheese
Mozzarella: a white, doughy type of cheese, this is sold floating in whey to keep it fresh. It has a delightful elastic texture which goes very stringy when it melts. Traditionally, the best mozzarella comes from Campania. When buying, make sure it is fresh, press gently between your finger and thumb – it should be very soft and wet.

Gorgonzola: a creamy, strongly-flavoured cows' milk blue cheese, this comes in two versions. The 'sweet' variety is matured for 60 days, while the more 'natural' version is matured for up to 100 days. It is delicious melted with milk and butter and used as a sauce on pasta.

Groviera: this is the Italian version of Gruyère and is practically identical.

Mascarpone: a very creamy, white cheese made from soured cows' milk.

Pecorino: this is reputed to be the oldest of all the Italian cheeses. It is a hard, grating ewes' milk cheese. The original version, known as Pecorino Romano, has a black rind. It is used a lot in pasta dishes, grated over the finished dish, but is also delicious with bread, fruit and cured meats. It has a very strong, piquant flavour and a characteristically pungent smell.

Ricotta: a white, slightly crumbly cheese with a wet texture typical of fresh cheeses.

Parmesan (Parmigiano Reggiano): this is made from unpasteurised skimmed milk from hillside-grazed cattle. It is matured for at least two, usually three years and is a completely naturally produced cheese. It is best bought in a wedge and freshly grated.

Cured or preserved meats (Salumi)
Prosciutto crudo: often mistakenly called Parma ham, it is, in fact, air- and salt-cured leg of pork. The dark red to pale pink paper-thin slices have a strip of soft fat down one side.

Pancetta: this is Italian bacon, made with the belly of the pig. It is a great deal fattier than English bacon and is usually cubed for use in cooking. Unlike prosciutto crudo, it is not usually eaten raw. It can be bought smoked and unsmoked.

Olive oil
Virgin olive oil is divided into several categories dependent on the the level of acidity in the oil – that with the lowest acidity being the most highly prized and most expensive. The top category 'extra virgin', from the first pressing of the pulp of high grade olives at a low temperature, has a maximum acidity of one per cent. This is followed by 'virgin' olive oil with a maximum of two per cent. Anything labelled 'pure' will undoubtedly be refined, be from a third or fourth pressing using heat as well as mechanical means to extract the oil and contain a percentage of virgin olive oil. 'Light' olive oil is produced by the last pressing and has a very mild flavour. For cooking buy an olive oil with a relatively mild flavour. Stronger flavoured oils are best for dressing salads.

Olives
Olives are among the world's oldest fruits and have been cultivated in the Mediterranean region since about 3000BC. They are bitter and inedible when picked and need to be cured before eating. Italy produces both large and small olives, usually black: the slightly acid Liguria, the salty Lugano, the mild Ponentine and the dry, wrinkled Gaeta.

Green olives: these are picked and processed when unripe, often pickled with herbs and spices and sold stuffed with slivers of red pepper or almonds.

Black olives: picked fully ripe, they are then cured to achieve the jet black finish. They are sold with their stones.

Pasta

At the last count there were more than 600 pasta shapes on the market and the number is growing but your problems don't end there.

Durum wheat pasta: this lies at the basis of all Italian food. No Italian household is ever without at least six packets in various shapes. It must be of good quality and kept sealed until required. You can tell the quality is good by checking the colour and texture: rich yellow and with a slight spring about it. When you plunge it into the boiling water the water should remain clear – not cloudy.

Fresh home-made pasta: made with egg and flour this is saved for special occasions.

Fresh commercially-made pasta: made with flour and water it may have eggs added to the dough. Fresh commercially-made pasta which contains eggs, pasta all'uovo, can also be bought dried as tagliatelle, lasagne, cannelloni and so on.

Unless fresh pasta is made well, you are better off sticking to the durum wheat factory-made varieties. Always cook pasta until al dente, that is 'firm to the bite' and not beyond.

Pulses

Borlotti beans: oval, quite plump with a thin, pinkish pale brown skin, deep maroon streaks and a bitter-sweet flavour. If you are lucky enough to find fresh beans, simply shell like peas and cook. There is no need for pre-soaking or boiling.

Cannellini beans: creamy-white, fairly slender with an elongated kidney bean shape, these have a fluffy texture when cooked.

Tomatoes

Beefsteak tomatoes: along with marmande tomatoes these are extra large and can weigh up to 450g/1lb. These are used in salads for their texture. Look for firm, deep red fruit.

Marmande tomatoes: from Provence, France and Morroco these should be snapped up. As with beefsteak tomatoes, a pale colour indicates the flavour is equally pallid.

Plum tomatoes: deep, bright red, very smooth and oval, these have the best flavour for sauces and soups. They have a denser, flesh than round varieties and are the most often canned variety.

EQUIPMENT

Ladles

These come in many sizes and are used for pouring liquids, skimming stocks, and sauces. Chose one with a hooked or pierced handle for easy storage.

Mezzaluna

An Italian two-handled, crescent-shaped chopping blade which can be used with a chopping board to chop herbs, vegetables and meat to the required degree of fineness. Double and triple-bladed mezzalunas are also available.

Pestle and mortar

The pestle is the pounding instrument, the mortar the container in which the food is pounded and worked round and round until reduced to a paste or powder. They can be made of wood, stone, porcelain, glass and marble and should be very heavy, so that the weight does some of the work. The Genoese will tell you that the most vital point about Pesto is the instruments used to make it – you should have a marble mortar with a wooden pestle.

1. Sage
2. Olive oi
3. Black olives
4. Beef tomato
5. Mascarpone
6. Ricotta
7. Cannellini beans
8. Risotto rice
9. Chick peas
10. Sardines
11. Passata
12. Pesto
13. Borlotti beans
14. Prosciutto
15. Speck
16. Pancetta
17. Anchovies
18. Mozzarella
19. Boudoir biscuits
20. Pine nuts
21. Fennel seeds
22. Pecorino
23. Fusilli pasta
24. Farfalle pasta
25. Penne pasta
26. Basil

1. Ladles
2. Pizza cutter
3. Pasta bowl
4. Pizza tins
5. Colander
6. Pasta tosser
7. Pasta server
8. Olive pitter
9. Risotto pan
10. Mezzaluna
11. Pizza plate
12. Pizza server
13. Meat mallet
14. Parmesan graters
15. Marble pestle and mortar
16. Wooden pestle and mortar

Antipasti

BLACK OLIVE PATE (PATE OLIVE NERE) ⓥ

Served with ice-cold, fairly acidic white wine to offset the slightly cloying flavour of the olives, this makes a delicious snack to savour before the meal. It is important to use juicy olives with plenty of flavour.

Serves 8

225g/8oz pitted black olives

juice and grated rind of ½ lemon, strained

1 large tbsp best quality olive oil

55g/2oz unsalted butter, softened

20g/¾oz very fresh white breadcrumbs (See Tip, page 51)

pinch of salt

generous grinding of black pepper

lightly toasted thin slices of bread, with a sheen of olive oil, to serve

1 Chop the olives finely, then put through a mincer two or three times using the finest blade. Or whizz in a food processor, at high speed, for 30 seconds.

2 Stir in the lemon juice and olive oil, then the remaining ingredients until light and fluffy. Check seasoning and chill for a minimum of 3 hours.

Nutrition notes per serving: *99 calories, Protein 1g, Carbohydrate 1g, Fat 10g, Saturated fat 4g, Fibre 1g, Added sugar none, Salt 1.77g.*

TIP

Many Italians like to add aubergine pulp to the mixture during the summer months. Instead of 225g/8oz olives, use 115g/4oz olives and 115g/4oz aubergines. Purée the olives, slice the aubergines and grill until dry and papery. Push the aubergines through a sieve or whizz in a processor to a smooth purée. Mix with the olive purée, then continue as above.

CAPRESE SALAD (LA CAPRESE) ⓥ

Probably the second most popular of all Italian antipasti after prosciutto crudo, this has been much maligned and betrayed since its original conception.

Serves 6

4 large marmande or beefsteak tomatoes, not too ripe

handful of fresh basil leaves

2 large mozzarella cheeses or 4 small ones

salt, to taste

1 tbsp olive oil

1 Slice the tomatoes evenly and arrange on a plate, then place a basil leaf on each tomato slice. (The amount of basil used is entirely up to personal preference.)

2 Cut the mozzarella into slices the same size as the tomato slices and lay one slice of cheese on each tomato. Sprinkle with salt, then pour over a little olive oil. Serve at once or chill for no longer than 30 minutes.

Nutrition notes per serving: *136 calories, Protein 9g, Carbohydrate 4g, Fat 9g, Saturated fat 5g, Fibre 1g, Added sugar none, Salt 0.71g.*

NELLO'S BAKED AUBERGINES WITH TOMATO AND MOZZARELLA (LA PARMIGIANA DI MELANZANE DI NELLO) Ⓥ

My thanks go to Nello and Vera Oliviero from the bay of Positano near Naples for teaching me how to make this dish.

Serves 4

about 300ml/½ pint oil

2 aubergines, cut lengthways into 1cm/½in thick slices

225ml/8fl oz cold Basic tomato sauce (page 62)

115g/4oz mozzarella, sliced (See Tip)

115g/4oz Parmesan, grated

about 12 fresh basil leaves, torn

1 Preheat the oven to 375F/190C/Gas 5. Heat the oil and fry the aubergine slices until golden, then drain thoroughly on kitchen paper.

2 Cover the base of a 20cm/8in baking dish with about two tablespoons of tomato sauce and top with a layer of aubergines, making sure they all point in the same direction. Cover with a layer of mozzarella, a layer of tomato sauce, a layer of Parmesan and a few basil leaves. Repeat layering, finishing with a thickish layer of tomato sauce, cheese and basil. Bake for 20–25 minutes and serve just warm or cold.

Nutrition notes per serving: *840 calories, Protein 22g, Carbohydrate 10g, Fat 80g, Saturated fat 19g, Fibre 5g, Added sugar none, Salt 1.84g.*

TIP

The best mozzarella is Mozzarella di Bufala which, as the name suggests, is made with buffalo milk. It is expensive and not always easy to find. The more common and widely available variety is made with cows' milk.

CAULIFLOWER FRITTERS (COTOLETTE DI CAVOLFIORE) Ⓥ

This dish, from Turin in Piedmont, is a delicious change from smothering a boiled cauliflower in a cheese sauce. It is wonderful with other fried dishes or served on its own.

Serves 4

8 fist-sized cauliflower florets

salt

8 walnut-sized chunks of cheese (mozzarella, Gorgonzola or anything which will melt and go gooey)

3 eggs

6 tbsp fresh breadcrumbs (See Tip, page 51)

oil for deep-frying

1 Boil the cauliflower in salted water for 4 minutes or until just tender. Drain and dry carefully. When cool enough to handle, insert a piece of cheese inside each floret, pushing it among the stalks to prevent it from falling out.

2 Beat the eggs with a pinch of salt. Spread the breadcrumbs on a plate. Heat the oil until a piece of bread dropped into it sizzles instantly.

3 Dip each floret into the egg, then into the breadcrumbs and deep-fry until crisp and golden. Drain on kitchen paper and serve.

Nutrition notes per serving: *352 calories, Protein 20g, Carbohydrate 10g, Fat 26g, Saturated fat 8g, Fibre 2g, Added sugar none, Salt 1.22g.*

Soups

COURGETTE SOUP (MINESTRA DI ZUCCHINE)

I adore this light and nourishing soup with its intense herby taste.

Serves 6

2 large onions, finely chopped

5 tbsp olive oil

6 large courgettes, cubed

small bunch mixed fresh herbs

700ml/1¼ pints Chicken stock (page 62)

2 eggs, beaten

salt and freshly ground black pepper

55g/2oz Parmesan , freshly grated

1 Fry the onions in the oil in a large pan for 5 minutes or until the onions are transparent. Stir in the courgettes, then the herbs, tied together in a bunch. Add the stock, bring to the boil, cover and simmer for 30 minutes or until the courgettes are pulpy.

2 Remove the pan from the heat and take out the herbs. Stir in the eggs and whisk them through the soup. Season and serve with grated cheese.

Nutrition notes per serving: *188 calories, Protein 8g, Carbohydrate 6g, Fat 15g, Saturated fat 4g, Fibre 2g, Added sugar none, Salt 0.87g.*

MINESTRONE Ⓥ

You can omit the pasta or rice for a much less filling soup.

Serves 6

250g/9oz dried borlotti or cannellini beans, soaked overnight

3 tbsp olive oil

1 onion, finely chopped

1 garlic clove, finely chopped

3 sticks celery, finely chopped

500g/1lb 2oz fresh spinach, chopped

2 courgettes, cut into tiny cubes

2 carrots, finely chopped

2 medium potatoes, quartered

2 small tomatoes, skinned, seeded and chopped

200g/7oz small pasta

salt and freshly ground black pepper

85g/3oz Parmesan, freshly grated

1 Drain and rinse the beans, place in a pan with fresh water, bring to the boil and boil rapidly for 5 minutes, then drain.

2 Meanwhile, place the oil, onion and garlic in a large pan and gently fry for 8 minutes or until soft. Add the vegetables, stir and cook for 10 minutes or until heated through and softened.

3 Add 1.4 litres/2½ pints of water, bring to the boil, cover and simmer gently for 1 hour. Add the beans, cover and simmer for a further 1 hour until the beans are soft. Add the pasta and boil for 7 minutes until tender. Season to taste, and serve hot or at room temperature with Parmesan.

Nutrition notes per serving: *412 calories, Protein 20g, Carbohydrate 59g, Fat 12g, Saturated fat 4g, Fibre 11g, Added sugar none, Salt 0.97g.*

TIP

Reduce the cooking time of this soup by using canned borlotti or cannellini beans. Drain, then add to the soup at the same time as the water.

Risotto

MIXED VEGETABLE RISOTTO
(RISOTTO ALLE VERDURE MISTE) Ⓥ

This is delightfully fresh and light and ideal for vegetarians. It is absolutely no good trying to make this marvellous creamy, sumptuous dish with long grain rice. Ideally, the very best variety of rice with which to make risotto is a very large-grained type called Carnaroli. The larger grains make absorption of flavour much better and improve the texture of the finished dish. However, it is almost impossible to get hold of even in Italy, and it is incredibly expensive. Arborio, which is widely available, is the next best type of rice. Italian risotto rice or Risotto rice, on sale in most major supermarkets, can also be used.

Serves 6

85g/3oz unsalted butter

1 onion, chopped

1 carrot, finely chopped

1 courgette, peeled and finely chopped

1 stick celery, finely chopped

4 tbsp shelled fresh peas or frozen petits pois

1 cos lettuce heart, shredded

1 plum tomato, skinned, seeded and chopped

500g/1lb 2oz risotto rice

1.7 litres/3 pints vegetable stock (See Tip), kept just below boiling point

salt and freshly ground black pepper

85g/3oz Parmesan, freshly grated

1 Melt the butter in a large heavy-based pan and gently fry the vegetables for 5 minutes or until soft. Add all the rice in one go and stir until it is heated through and shining. Add a ladleful of stock, stir until it has been absorbed, then add some more.

2 Add small amounts of stock and always wait for the rice to absorb it before adding any more. Continue in this way for 20 minutes or until the rice is swollen but still firm in the middle. Season and stir in the Parmesan. Remove from the heat, cover and stand for 3 minutes before serving.

Nutrition notes per serving: *505 calories, Protein 13g, Carbohydrate 78g, Fat 18g, Saturated fat 11g, Fibre 2g, Added sugar none, Salt 1.53g.*

TIP

For a well-flavoured vegetable stock, place two lettuce hearts, two halved carrots, one quartered onion, two halved celery sticks, two halved tomatoes, eight parsley stalks, one quartered medium leek, a handful of fresh spinach and a shredded cabbage leaf in a large pan. Add 1.2 litres/2 pints of cold water and two pinches of salt and stir once. Place over a medium heat and bring to the boil slowly, then simmer for 1½ hours. Remove from the heat and cool completely, then strain into a bowl or jug. It will keep in the fridge for up to five days. Makes about 850ml/1½ pints.

RISOTTO WITH CHICKEN AND PEAS
(RISOTTO AL POLLO E PISELLINI)

I have some very special and fond memories about risotto because it was the first thing I ever learned to make. I was a very tiny girl, only three or four, and I had to stand on a big chair next to my friend as he made it. Beppino comes from Vicenza and used to be a chef at one of the top restaurants in Milan, so you could say he had risotto in his blood, as both these areas are famous for producing excellent risottos. With immense patience, he would explain to me just how to stir the grains as he poured in the hot stock. He would teach me how much it needs to stick on the bottom of the pot and how the surface had to ripple like the sea touched by gentle breezes. *'Deve fare l'onda,'* he would say, *'Guarda l'onda, se no non é risotto.'* 'It must make a wave. Watch the wave or else it isn't risotto.' He also taught me that anything from a humble courgette to an exotic wild mushroom can turn a simple risotto into something quite amazing, the sort of everlasting flavour impression which you can recall at any time. I will never be able to cook or eat risotto again without remembering that kitchen, that chair and my friend Beppino. This is one of my children's favourite risottos. It is a very good way of using up leftover chicken and is traditionally served quite liquid and runny.

Serves 6

85g/3oz unsalted butter

½ onion, chopped

250g cooked chicken, coarsely chopped

250g/9oz shelled fresh peas or frozen petits pois

500g/1lb 2oz risotto rice

1.7 litres/3 pints Chicken stock (page 62), kept just below boiling point

85g/3oz Parmesan, freshly grated

salt and freshly ground black pepper

1 Melt half the butter and fry the onion for 5 minutes or until soft and transparent. Add the chicken and peas and stir, carefully, over a low heat for 5 minutes. Add all the rice in one go and stir it around until it is heated through and shining. Add a ladleful of stock and stir until it has been absorbed, then add more.

2 Add small amounts of stock and always wait for the rice to absorb it before adding any more. Continue in this way for 20 minutes or until the rice is swollen but still firm in the middle.

3 Stir in the the remaining butter and three-quarters of the Parmesan, then season. Remove from the heat, cover and leave to stand for 3 minutes. Serve sprinkled with the remaining Parmesan.

Nutrition notes per serving: *575 calories, Protein 26g, Carbohydrate 78g, Fat 20g, Saturated fat 11g, Fibre 3g, Added sugar none, Salt 1.58g.*

TIP

The basic method of making risotto is always the same, all that changes are the extra ingredients. It is important to stir constantly after adding the rice and to have the stock hot, so that the risotto never drops in temperature while cooking.

Pasta

SPRINGTIME PENNE
(PENNE PRIMAVERA)

Traditionally, pasta asciutta, that is pasta with a sauce which is tossed together in a bowl, as opposed to pasta in a baked dish or in a soup, is served after the antipasto and before the main course. Nowadays, our appetites are getting smaller and demands for large, long meals are rarer, so very often a dish of pasta, perhaps served with salad, constitutes an entire meal. This recipe makes a good lunch-time dish with plenty of different textures and flavours. If you are using fresh pasta, it requires a much shorter cooking time. Refer to packet instructions. To help stop pasta sticking while it is cooking, add a tablespoon of olive oil to the boiling water and stir occasionally. Test by tasting, the bigger and thicker it is, the longer it will take.

Serves 6

1 small onion, finely chopped

1 carrot, finely chopped

1 stick celery, finely chopped

125ml/4fl oz olive oil

300g coarsely minced beef

salt and freshly ground black pepper

175ml/6fl oz beef stock

140g/5oz grilled peppers, sliced or canned peppers

200g/7oz shelled fresh peas or frozen petits pois

300g can chopped tomatoes

500g/1lb 2oz penne

1   Fry the onion, carrot and celery gently in the oil for 5 minutes or until soft. Add the beef and fry until browned all over. Season to taste and cook for a further 10 minutes, gradually adding a little stock.

2   Stir in the peppers and peas and bring to a bubbling simmer. Stir in the tomatoes, bring to a simmer, cover and simmer for 40 minutes. Check seasoning and add more stock, if necessary.

3   Bring a large pan of salted water to a rolling boil, toss in the penne and give it one good stir. Cover the pan and bring back to the boil. Remove the lid and cook until al dente. Check the instructions on the packet as brands vary but 10 minutes should be about right.

4   Drain the penne thoroughly and return to the warm pan, pour over half the sauce and toss together thoroughly. Transfer to a warm serving bowl, cover with remaining sauce and serve.

Nutrition notes per serving: *538 calories, Protein 24g, Carbohydrate 71g, Fat 20g, Saturated fat 4g, Fibre 5g, Added sugar none, Salt 0.43g.*

TIP

One of the questions I am often asked is what sauce to put with what shape of pasta. I can only say that this decision is down to trial and error. Certain shapes marry certain sauces much better than others. The general rule of thumb is that delicately flavoured, light sauces go best with delicate pasta shapes, whether they be ribbon-shaped or short. The more rich, chunky sauces, particularly those which contain meat or game, tend to sit better with bigger, chunkier pasta shapes. But there are simply no hard-and-fast rules.

SPAGHETTI CARBONARA (SPAGHETTI ALLA CARBONARA)

This very simple and classic pasta dish works best with spaghetti although you can use any other pasta shape, if you prefer.

Serves 6

8 rashers pancetta (See Tip) or streaky bacon

4 eggs, thoroughly beaten

40g/1½oz Parmesan, freshly grated

coarse sea salt

freshly ground black pepper (optional)

2 tbsp double cream (optional)

500g/1lb 2oz spaghetti

1   Preheat the grill to medium and place the pancetta under until cooked through. Beat the eggs with the Parmesan, a pinch of salt, plenty of pepper and the cream, if using. Remove the pancetta from the grill, cut off and reserve the fat. Cut the pancetta into small pieces using scissors and keep warm.

2   Bring a large pan of salted water to a rolling boil, fold in the spaghetti and give it one good stir. Add a large pinch of sea salt, cover the pan and return to the boil. Remove the lid and give it another good stir, then cook until al dente. Check the packet instructions but 7 minutes should be about right.

3   Meanwhile, reheat the pancetta with its fat, very slowly in a frying pan. Drain the spaghetti thoroughly, then return to the warm pan. Pour over the eggs and toss together. Add the sizzling, crispy, hot pancetta, then serve.

Nutrition notes per serving: *525 calories, Protein 22g, Carbohydrate 62g, Fat 23g, Saturated fat 9g, Fibre 2g, Added sugar none, Salt 1.75g.*

TIP

Pancetta, an Italian salted raw belly of pork, looks like streaky bacon and can be bought in long rasher form or rolled up. It has a distinctive smoky flavour.

FUSILLI WITH TOMATO AND MOZZARELLA SAUCE (FUSILLI ALLA VESUVIANA) Ⓥ

In the Naples area, all plain tomato sauces are cooked for the least possible time, to keep the colour and fragrance intact.

Serves 4

400g/14oz fusilli or other dried durum wheat pasta

salt and freshly ground black pepper

100ml/3½fl oz olive oil

400g/14oz fresh, ripe tomatoes or 400g can chopped tomatoes

115g/4oz mozzarella, thinly sliced

55g/2oz pecorino cheese, grated

generous pinch dried oregano

1   Preheat the oven to 450F/230C/Gas 8. Bring a large pan of salted water to a rolling boil. Toss in the pasta, stir and cook until al dente. Check the instructions on the packet for timing, as brands vary.

2   Meanwhile, place the olive oil, tomatoes, mozzarella, pecorino, oregano and salt and pepper in a pan. Mix together and cook fast over a high heat for the same amount of time as it takes for the pasta to cook.

3   Drain the pasta and return to the warm pan, pour over the sauce and mix well. Transfer to an ovenproof dish and bake for 5 minutes before serving.

Nutrition notes per serving: *668 calories, Protein 26g, Carbohydrate 77g, Fat 31g, Saturated fat 10g, Fibre 4g, Added sugar none, Salt 1.18g.*

FARFALLE WITH RICOTTA (FARFALLE ALLA RICOTTA) ⓥ

You can use any shape for this very simple, delicately flavoured dish which is ideal for children. I like to serve this in summer as a lunch-time treat.

Serves 4

300g/10½oz ricotta cheese

1 shallot, finely chopped

1 stick celery, finely chopped

3-4 tbsp milk

salt and freshly ground black pepper

400g/14oz farfalle or other pasta shape

55g/2oz unsalted butter

55g/2oz Parmesan, freshly grated (optional)

3 tsp chopped fresh parsley or snipped chives

1   Mash the ricotta with the shallot and celery, adding the milk gradually to make a smooth, creamy paste, then season to taste.

2   Meanwhile, bring a large pan of salted water to a rolling boil, toss in the farfalle and give it one good stir. Cover the pan, and return to the boil. Remove the lid and cook until al dente. Check the instructions on the packet as brands vary but 8 minutes should be about right. Drain the pasta, but not too thoroughly and return to the warm pan.

3   Add the butter to the pan and toss together thoroughly, then add the ricotta sauce and toss again. Add the Parmesan, if using, and serve sprinkled with fresh parsley or chives.

Nutrition notes per serving: *626 calories, Protein 25g, Carbohydrate 77g, Fat 26g, Saturated fat 11g, Fibre 3g, Added sugar none, Salt 0.87g.*

VERMICELLI WITH PEPPERS AND AUBERGINES
(VERMICELLI CON PEPERONI E MELANZANE) ⓥ

Use juicy peppers and firm aubergines for this dish. Add as much fresh basil as you like.

Serves 4

3 garlic cloves, chopped

1 small onion, chopped

4 tbsp olive oil

1 large aubergine, peeled and cubed

2 large peppers, seeded and cubed

250g/9oz passata (See Tip)

salt and freshly ground black pepper

6 fresh basil leaves, torn into small pieces

400g/14oz vermicelli

1   Fry the garlic and onion in the oil for about 5 minutes or until soft. Add the aubergine and peppers and cook for 8 minutes. Stir in the passata and season to taste. Cover loosely and simmer for 20 minutes, stirring frequently. Stir in the basil, cover and remove from the heat. Leave to one side so that the flavour of the basil develops in the heat of the sauce.

2   Bring a large pan of salted water to a rolling boil, toss in the vermicelli and give it one good stir. Cover the pan and return to the boil. Remove the lid and cook until al dente. Check the instructions on the packet as brands vary but 5 minutes should be about right. Drain the vermicelli thoroughly and return to the warm pan. Pour over the sauce, toss together and serve.

Nutrition notes per serving: *489 calories, Protein 12g, Carbohydrate 89g, Fat 12g, Saturated fat 2g, Fibre 4g, Added sugar 2g, Salt 0.60g.*

TIP

Passata (sieved tomatoes) is sold in jars and cartons. If you cannot find any, simply push canned tomatoes through a sieve. You can also add a little tomato purée for extra density of flavour and texture.

Pizza

FOUR-SEASON PIZZA
(PIZZA ALLE 4 STAGIONI)

This is one pizza recipe where you really can use your imagination. The idea is to divide a large pizza into quarters and put something different on each quarter.

Serves 4

1 quantity Pizza dough (page 62)

FIRST QUARTER
55g/2oz mozzarella, chopped
2 thin slices prosciutto crudo
1 tbsp olive oil

SECOND QUARTER
3 tbsp passata (See Tip, page 27)
1 garlic clove, finely chopped
large pinch dried oregano
salt and freshly ground black pepper
1 tbsp olive oil

THIRD QUARTER
3 tbsp passata (See Tip, page 27)
2 tbsp assorted cooked shellfish,
such as mussels, clams, prawns
1 tbsp olive oil
1 tbsp chopped fresh parsley
salt and freshly ground black pepper

FOURTH QUARTER
2 tbsp passata (See Tip, page 27)
55g/2oz mushrooms, sliced
1 tbsp olive oil
55g/2oz mozzarella, chopped
salt and freshly ground black pepper

1 Preheat the oven to 475F/240C/Gas 9. Sprinkle the cheese on the first quarter, cover with prosciutto and drizzle over the oil.

2 Cover the second quarter with passata, sprinkle with garlic, oregano and seasoning, then sprinkle with olive oil.

3 Spread the third quarter with passata, scatter over the shellfish, then sprinkle with olive oil, parsley and seasoning.

4 Cover the last quarter with passata and scatter over the mushrooms. Sprinkle with olive oil, then cover with mozzarella and season. Bake for 10 minutes or until cooked through.

Nutrition notes per serving: *618 calories, Protein 24g, Carbohydrate 78g, Fat 25g, Saturated fat 7g, Fibre 4g, Added sugar 1g, Salt 2.13g.*

TIP

To Italians, the pizza base serves merely as a background for the topping. It should be thin and after being pushed and squashed into position with oiled hands to fill the tin, rubbed with a little more olive oil.

TRADITIONAL PIZZA TOPPINGS

The original pizza was invented by a backstreet Neapolitan baker, though sadly his name has gone unrecorded and has been forgotten. All toppings are based on a 4-person pizza.

Makes 4 pizzas

1 quantity Pizza dough (page 62)

THE MARINARA

8 tbsp passata (See Tip, page 27)

2 large pinches dried oregano

2–4 garlic cloves, chopped

1 tbsp finely chopped fresh basil (optional)

2 tbsp olive oil

salt and freshly ground black pepper

THE MARGHERITA

8 tbsp passata (See Tip, page 27)

115g/4oz mozzarella, chopped

large pinch dried oregano

8 fresh basil leaves, torn

salt and freshly ground black pepper

2 tbsp olive oil

THE NAPOLETANA

8 tbsp passata (See Tip, page 27)

85g/3oz mozzarella, chopped

40g/1½ oz canned anchovy fillets, drained and chopped or 40g/1½oz anchovy paste

2 tbsp olive oil

salt and freshly ground black pepper

MUSHROOM PIZZA

8 tbsp passata (See Tip, page 27)

85g/3oz mushrooms, peeled and thinly sliced

about 85g/3oz mozzarella, chopped

2 tbsp olive oil

salt and freshly ground black pepper

pinch dried oregano (optional)

1 Preheat the oven to 475F/240C/Gas 9. Spread the passata over the top of the pizza, leaving a 2.5cm/1in space around the edges. Scatter over chosen toppings, then sprinkle with olive oil and seasoning. Bake for 10 minutes, or until the crust is crisp and cooked through.

THE MARINARA (LA MARINARA) Ⓥ

This was the first pizza ever baked. Despite its name it has nothing whatsoever to do with seashores or marine life.

Nutrition notes per serving: *462 calories, Protein 13g, Carbohydrate 79g, Fat 13g, Saturated fat 2g, Fibre 3g, Added sugar 1g, Salt 1.04g.*

THE MARGHERITA (LA MARGHERITA) Ⓥ

This pizza was created in honour of Queen Margherita of Savoy.

Nutrition notes per serving: *547 calories, Protein 20g, Carbohydrate 78g, Fat 19g, Saturated fat 6g, Fibre 3g, Added sugar 1g, Salt 1.48g.*

THE NAPOLETANA (LA NAPOLETANA)

This is the only pizza that traditionally uses anchovy.

Nutrition notes per serving: *547 calories, Protein 20g, Carbohydrate 78g, Fat 19g, Saturated fat 5g, Fibre 3g, Added sugar 1g, Salt 2.37g.*

MUSHROOM PIZZA (PIZZA AI FUNGHI) Ⓥ

Nutrition notes per serving: *521 calories, Protein 18g, Carbohydrate 78g, Fat 17g, Saturated fat 5g, Fibre 4g, Added sugar 1g, Salt 1.37g.*

Meat

PIZZAIOLA STEAK
(COSTATA ALLA PIZZAIOLA)

To me this epitomises the style of Campanian cookery – Neapolitan in particular. Such is the Neapolitans' love of the brilliant red tomato, that in dishes such as this it is cooked as little as possible so as not to lose any of the bright colour, tangy flavour or scent. Naturally the dish is best made in its area of origin with freshly gathered, sun-warmed tomatoes, but it is still very good even when you use canned tomatoes or passata (See Tip, page 27). It is the quintessential Neapolitan dish – quick and easy, bright and colourful, versatile and delicious. It was cooked for me by a very charming friend made on my travels – the Neapolitan surgeon Nello Oliviero, who invited me to his home for lunch. I enjoyed a wonderful meal in the family's beautiful flat – the dining room in particular has a really spectacular view over the bay of Naples, and the basil came from Nello's herb garden on the terrace. In fact, so keen was he to have fresh basil that he had part of the terrace covered with glass to help it grow. He and his wife Vera also taught me how to make Nello's baked aubergines with tomato and mozzarella (page 15).

Serves 4

750g sirloin or rump steak, thinly sliced (See Tip)

6 tbsp olive oil

3 garlic cloves, crushed

750g canned tomatoes, sieved

2 tbsp chopped fresh parsley

3 tbsp chopped fresh basil

salt and freshly ground black pepper

1 Trim any gristle and fat off the meat, flatten as much as possible with a meat mallet and set aside. Heat the oil in a frying pan wide enough to take all the meat in a single layer, add the garlic and gently fry for 3 minutes.

2 Add the tomatoes, parsley and basil, stir and bring to the boil. Slip the meat into the tomato sauce and cook very quickly for 5 minutes or until the meat is done to your liking. Sprinkle with salt and plenty of pepper, then serve.

Nutrition notes per serving: *418 calories, Protein 41g, Carbohydrate 7g, Fat 25g, Saturated fat 6g, Fibre 2g, Added sugar none, Salt 0.73g.*

TIP

You can use any kind of meat, except lamb, for this dish. Thinly sliced veal or well-flattened skinned chicken breasts will cook most quickly.

MEATBALLS IN LEMON LEAVES
(POLPETTE NELLA FOGLIA DI LIMONE) ❄

Eleonora Consoli made these delicious meatballs for me at Lentini, cooking them on a grill laid over the embers of a lemon-wood fire. At Lentini there is no shortage of lemon trees, as they grow alongside the oranges and vines in wildly Sicilian, passionate profusion. In the UK it is less easy to find lemon trees (See Tip). The object of the leaves is to impart a vaguely lemony scent and flavour to the meat, but I have experimented with making the dish with no leaves and as long as you fry the meatballs in olive oil, squeeze lemon juice over and serve them hot, they are absolutely scrumptious.

Serves 4

400g minced veal, beef, turkey or chicken

115g/4oz dry breadcrumbs (See Tip, page 51)

115g/4oz caciocavallo or Parmesan cheese, grated

1 large egg

salt and freshly ground black pepper

3 tbsp chopped fresh parsley

lemon leaves (See Tip) or 6 tbsp olive oil plus the juice of ½ lemon and 1 tsp grated rind

1. Combine the meat, breadcrumbs, cheese, egg, salt, pepper and parsley together thoroughly, then gradually blend in half a wine glass of cold water. Mix with your hands for a few minutes, shape the mixture into small balls about the size of a large walnut, then press them slightly flat with your palms.

2. Sandwich each meatball between two lemon leaves, if using, securing with two wooden cocktail sticks.

3. Cook the meatballs over a moderate heat on a barbecue or under a grill until the leaves begin to burn slightly, turning them over after about 4 minutes. If you have no lemon leaves, fry the meatballs in the olive oil, drain on kitchen paper, then sprinkle with the lemon juice and grated rind.

Nutrition notes per serving: *331 calories, Protein 37g, Carbohydrate 14g, Fat 14g, Saturated fat 8g, Fibre 1g, Added sugar none, Salt 1.76g.*

❄ *Freeze the meatballs at the end of Step 1 before wrapping in the lemon leaves. Can be frozen for up to 1 month. To serve, defrost in the fridge, wrap in leaves, if using, then grill or barbecue.*

TIP

If you can't find lemon leaves, the branches of leaves attached to clementines or tangerines make a good substitute. The meatballs are also delicious grilled without the leaves but with extra zest and juice added to the mixture.

ESCALOPE WITH MOZZARELLA AND HAM
(SALTIMBOCCA)

All my family really love this quick and simple to prepare dish. I have also used flattened strips of pork loin which taste very good. To flatten meat use a meat mallet. Or place between two sheets of non-stick baking paper or plastic film and hit with a rolling pin.

Serves 6

handful of fresh sage leaves
(See Tip)

600g veal or turkey escalopes,
trimmed and flattened

55g/2oz prosciutto crudo, sliced

55g/2oz unsalted butter

salt and freshly ground black pepper

85g/3oz mozzarella, thinly sliced

1   Place a sage leaf on top of each escalope. Cut the ham to size and lay the slices on top of the sage leaves.

2   Melt the butter in a wide frying pan and fry the meat for 1½ minutes on each side. Season to taste, then cover each escalope with a mozzarella slice. Cover the pan and increase the heat to maximum for about 1 minute to allow the mozzarella to start melting, then serve.

Nutrition notes per serving: *240 calories, Protein 28g, Carbohydrate 1g, Fat 14g, Saturated fat 8g, Fibre none, Added sugar none, Salt 1.11g.*

TIP

Here is the perfect recipe if you need an unusual and very tasty snack to serve with a glass of sparkling Prosecco or other wine before a meal. It is also an excellent way of using up sage leaves. Sandwich together, in pairs, 32 fresh sage leaves using two tablespoons of anchovy paste. Beat 40g/1½oz of plain white flour with five to six tablespoons of water to make a batter the consistency of double cream. Season to taste with salt. Beat one chilled egg white until stiff, then fold into the batter and dip in the sage leaf sandwiches to coat them. Heat 150ml/¼ pint of olive oil until sizzling and fry the sage leaf sandwiches for a few minutes until golden and crispy. Drain on kitchen paper and serve hot. Serves 4.

COUNTRY-STYLE ROAST LAMB
(ABBACCHIO ALLA CAMPAGNOLA) ✺

Lamb is something of a rarity in Italy except where it has been traditional to eat it because it was one of the few meats available. Especially around Easter, however, lamb does become more readily available. You'll probably be offered abbacchio and agnello. The former is an older animal up to a year old generally, and the latter is a very young baby lamb. Mutton is considered to be poisonous by certain people and is generally not eaten at all. As always with any kind of meat and whatever country you are in, the basic rules of freshness when buying meat are the same. It should have a pleasant smell, good even colouring, not too much blood (meat which has been insufficiently hung will drizzle blood everywhere), not too much fat and reasonable tenderness. It is very hard to tell if a piece of meat is going to be tender until it has been cooked, and I must say Italian meat is generally a lot less tender than I would like it to be. However, you're always safe with veal escalopes and long-cooked dishes such as casseroles and stews. The strong flavours of anchovies, garlic and caraway seeds make this a very special way of roasting lamb – delicious and very rustic.

Serves 6

1.25kg leg of lamb, boned

55g/2oz unsalted butter

2 tbsp olive oil

3 whole salted anchovies, boned, rinsed and dried (See Tip)

2 garlic cloves, peeled

1 tbsp caraway seeds

2–3 tbsp red wine vinegar

1 tbsp plain white flour

1–2 ladles of water or meat stock

1 Cut the lamb into large chunks about the size of a small child's fist. Wash carefully and pat dry with kitchen paper. Heat the butter and oil in a large pan, add the meat and brown all over.

2 Using a pestle and mortar, pound the anchovies to a purée with the garlic, caraway seeds and red wine vinegar.

3 Drain most of the fat off the meat, pour over the anchovy sauce and stir the meat to thoroughly flavour. Sprinkle with the flour, then add one ladleful of water or stock. Stir again, simmer for 40 minutes, adding more liquid if necessary, then serve.

Nutrition notes per serving: *550 calories, Protein 42g, Carbohydrate 4g, Fat 41g, Saturated fat 20g, Fibre1g, Added sugar none, Salt 0.70g.*

✺ *Cool quickly, then freeze. Can be frozen for up to 1 month. To serve, defrost in the fridge, then reheat until piping hot.*

TIP

You can buy salted anchovies in delicatessens. If you want to remove some of their saltiness soak in water or milk before filleting. Split and fillet the fish using a knife or even your thumbnail.

Poultry

PAN-ROASTED CHICKEN WITH SAGE

(POLLO ALLA SALVIA) ❄

Chicken, which used to be regarded as a rich man's delicacy, has long since become an everyday food for many people. I think this is as true in Italy as it is beyond her boundaries. Yet the humble chicken, with its reputation for eminent stupidity and its role of scapegoat in many different cultures, offers us meat which is low in fat, high in flavour and extremely adaptable and easy to cook in a thousand and one different ways. From the most basic roast chicken, boiled chicken, braised chicken or chicken cacciatora, chicken is at the root of Italian cooking. Chicken, or any other poultry for that matter, was traditionally served after the antipasto and the pasta course as the main course. A marvellously simple dish, this is very good served with carrots and mashed potatoes.

Serves 6

1 heaped tbsp unsalted butter

2 tbsp olive oil

6 large chicken joints, trimmed (See Tip)

1 large glass dry white wine

55g/2oz prosciutto crudo, cut into slivers

1 fresh sage sprig, roughly chopped

salt and freshly ground black pepper

1 Heat the butter and oil in a large frying pan and fry the chicken joints gently until dark brown all over. Drain off as much of the fat as possible, pour over the wine and boil off the alcohol for 2 minutes.

2 Sprinkle on the prosciutto and sage and season generously. Mix together thoroughly, cover and simmer gently for 45 minutes, basting occasionally with a little water if the chicken appears to be drying out before it is cooked, then serve.

Nutrition notes per serving: *445 calories, Protein 30g, Carbohydrate 1g, Fat 35g, Saturated fat 11g, Fibre none, Added sugar none, Salt 0.88g.*

❄ *Cool quickly, then freeze. Can be frozen for up to 1 month. To serve, defrost in the fridge, then reheat until piping hot.*

TIP

It is usually cheaper to buy a whole chicken and cut it up yourself. This way you get the whole carcase which can be used to make a good stock for use in soups, sauces and casseroles.

BRAISED CHICKEN WITH OLIVES
(POLLO ALLA CACCIATORA) ⊛

I love the strong flavour of this really simple to make dish. It tastes excellent with a fresh green salad and roast potatoes. I can only say that to eat fresh, honestly free-range chicken is an experience well worth striving for. I enjoy keeping my chickens enormously. Apart from anything else, they will eat all the cooking scraps and are, therefore, a marvellously easy way of recycling some of my household waste. There is no doubt in my mind that an animal that is allowed to live freely will result in a meat with far better flavour and texture. After all, you are what you eat, even if you are only a chicken.

Serves 6

3 tbsp olive oil

3 garlic cloves, lightly crushed

1kg chicken joints

½ tumbler dry white wine

2 tbsp white wine vinegar

20 whole pitted black olives (See Tip)

20 pitted black olives, chopped

1 tbsp anchovy paste

salt and freshly ground black pepper

1   Heat the oil and garlic in a shallow pan until the garlic is golden brown. Add the chicken joints and brown them all over. Add the wine and wine vinegar and boil off the alcohol for 2 minutes.

2   Stir in all the olives, the anchovy paste and season to taste. Cover and simmer for 25 minutes or until the chicken is cooked through, stirring and adding a little water, from time to time, to prevent the chicken from drying out or sticking to the pan. Test the chicken is cooked by piercing with a skewer or the point of a knife, the juices should run clear.

Nutrition notes per serving: *422 calories, Protein 27g, Carbohydrate 1g, Fat 35g, Saturated fat 9g, Fibre 1g, Added sugar none, Salt 1.62g.*

⊛ *Cool quickly, then freeze. Can be frozen for up to 1 month. To serve, defrost in the fridge, then reheat until piping hot.*

TIP

To stone olives: strain any liquid and use an olive pitter or cherry stoner. Alternatively, the olive can be split with the point of a knife and the stone prised out. You can buy pitted olives, with the stones already removed, if you prefer.

ROMAN CHICKEN STEW
(POLLO GRILLETTATO ALLA ROMANA) ⊛

The Lazio is one of the few areas where chicken is eaten in any quantity worth mentioning – 'Alas,' say the Italian cardiologists, 'not enough white meat is eaten in this country!' On the whole, dishes of this region tend to be full of very strong flavours, quite greasy and heavy – not food for the faint-hearted. This dish would traditionally be served with popular local vegetables: peas, artichokes, salads like puntarelle, peppers, broad beans, broccoli and cabbages of many different kinds, as well as the carefully picked wild vegetables, gathered at the roadside by people who know what they are looking for.

Serves 4–6

1 x 1.3kg chicken, jointed

55g/2oz prosciutto crudo, coarsely chopped

4 tbsp chopped fresh parsley

3 tbsp olive oil

1 large glass white wine

1 large garlic clove, chopped

large pinch dried marjoram

450g canned tomatoes, drained and seeded

½ chicken stock cube or 4 tbsp very concentrated Chicken stock (page 62)

salt and freshly ground black pepper

8 slices from a large French stick, cut at an angle to give the largest possible slice, to serve

1 Wash and dry the chicken joints. Fry the prosciutto and parsley together in the oil for 5 minutes over a low heat. Add the chicken joints, raise the heat and brown them well all over.

2 Sprinkle over the wine, then add the garlic and marjoram. Add the tomatoes, stock cube or stock and seasoning. Cover the pan and simmer for 30 minutes, stirring occasionally.

3 Toast the bread and arrange around the edge of a warmed serving plate. Place the chicken in the centre of the circle, pour over the sauce and serve.

Nutrition notes per serving for four: *766 calories, Protein 47g, Carbohydrate 32g, Fat 48g, Saturated fat 13g, Fibre 2g, Added sugar none, Salt 2.20g.*

⊛ *Cool quickly, then freeze at the end of Step 2. Can be frozen for up to 1 month. To serve, defrost in the fridge, then reheat until piping hot and serve with toasted French bread.*

TIP

Rabbit can be cooked in exactly the same way for an equally delicious dish.

Fish

SALMON WITH PESTO
(SALMONE AL PESTO)

Pesto is a fresh basil sauce made with garlic, pine nuts, olive oil, Parmesan cheese and seasoning. You can use it on any pasta shape you like, stir it into soups, pour it over boiled potatoes or use as a dip with breadsticks. In this recipe it complements fresh salmon. You can cook the fish by covering it in pesto and wrapping in foil. Place the foil parcels under the grill or in a 400F/200C/Gas 6 preheated oven for 5–6 minutes, then serve the parcels for your guests to unwrap.

Serves 6

12 very small salmon tail fillets or salmon steaks

1 jar very good quality pesto sauce (See Tip)

1 wine glass dry white wine

3 tbsp olive oil

salt and freshly ground black pepper

fresh basil leaves, to garnish

1 Place the fish in a shallow bowl. Whisk the pesto with the wine and oil until the sauce has completely emulsified. Pour over the fish and season to taste. Leave to marinate in a cool place, not the fridge, for about 5 hours, turning the fish occasionally, so it absorbs the flavours.

2 Heat a skillet or heavy non-stick pan rubbed lightly with oil. Remove the fish from the marinade with a slotted spoon and cook briefly for about 4 minutes on each side, turning frequently. While the fish is cooking, spoon over the pesto so that by the time the fish is cooked, all the sauce is in the pan. Transfer to a warmed serving plate and garnish.

Nutrition notes per serving: *384 calories, Protein 21g, Carbohydrate 1g, Fat 32g, Saturated fat 7g, Fibre 1g, Added sugar none, Salt 1.28g.*

TIP

If you prefer you can make your own pesto. It is one of my very favourite sauces. There are many variations on the basic sauce: some people use walnuts, others pine nuts; I have seen some cooks put creamy milk junket into the sauce and others who chop smoked bacon very finely and stir it in. What is essential is a large amount of fresh basil; and by this I mean at least four handfuls for the quantities given, more if possible. If you are using a pestle and mortar, remember to press the basil leaves against the sides; do not bang downwards as usual. You can also makes it in a food processor. Place 36 washed and dried fresh basil leaves, a large pinch of rock salt and two halved garlic cloves into the mortar or food processor and reduce to a smooth green purée. Blend in one handful of pine nuts and two tablespoons of freshly grated Parmesan cheese. Add about half a wine glass of olive oil, a little at a time, until you have a smooth, creamy texture. Season with salt and freshly ground black pepper and use as required. Makes enough to dress 500g/1lb 2oz pasta.

BAKED SARDINES WITH FENNEL SEEDS
(SARDE AL FINOCCHIO)

The tastes of fennel and sardine seem almost made for one another, they really set each other off beautifully. Although I have specified fresh sardines, I realise they may be hard to find and you may need to opt for the frozen variety.

Serves 6

1 very large onion, thinly sliced

6 tbsp olive oil

1 large wine glass dry red wine

500g/1lb 2oz passata (See Tip, page 27)

salt and freshly ground black papper

140g/5oz dried breadcrumbs (See Tip, page 51)

2 heaped tbsp fennel seeds, crushed

900g/2lb fresh sardines, scaled, gutted, boned and headless (See Tip)

1   Preheat the oven to 350F/180C/Gas 4. Blanch the onion in boiling water for 30 seconds, then drain and transfer to cold water. Drain and dry thoroughly on kitchen paper.

2   Heat half the oil and gently fry the onion for 6 minutes or until golden brown. Add the wine and boil off the alcohol for 2 minutes. Stir in the passata, season to taste, then bring to the boil, cover and simmer for 15 minutes.

3   Meanwhile, mix together the breadcrumbs and fennel seeds. Spoon half the tomato sauce over the base of an ovenproof dish. Top with half the sardines, then make a layer using half the breadcrumbs. Repeat with more sauce, sardines and breadcrumbs. Drizzle over the remaining oil and bake for 30 minutes before serving.

Nutrition notes per serving: *354 calories, Protein 24g, Carbohydrate 22g, Fat 18g, Saturated fat 3g, Fibre 1g, Added sugar 3g, Salt 1.17g.*

TIP

To clean fresh sardines: first, carefully remove the scales. Sardines have very tender flesh so it is easy to tear it. Lay the fish on a sheet of newspaper and scrape the scales away with the blunt side of a knife from the tail end towards the head. Slit the belly open with scissors and ease out the innards. Wash and dry the gutted fish and hold it firmly in your hand, belly-side up. With your other hand, grip the head with your thumb and forefinger. Pull the head down through the fish towards you, removing the spine and all the bones, so that you end up with a neat, flat fish. Wash and pat dry with kitchen paper. It is now ready to cook. For a deliciously quick dish I like to coat sardines in beaten egg and breadcrumbs and fry them in a little oil until crisp and golden. After draining on kitchen paper, serve with lemon wedges to cut through the inevitable oiliness. Because they are such an oily fish, they should be cooked with a minimum of oil or fat of any kind. They are also ideally suited to grilling because they are protected by their skin which keeps the inside moist and forms a natural crust on the outside. If you are grilling them, they only need to be gutted and washed, not boned.

PAN-FRIED TROUT WITH MUSHROOMS AND ONIONS
(TROTA ALLA SAVOIARDA)

Fresh farmed trout is as popular in Italy as it is elsewhere and because it has a relatively bland flavour, a good firm flesh and a pleasant appearance, it seems to have become the most adaptable and flexible of fish – rather like the chicken of the fish world. Although trout farms breed fish which is available all year round, it is not at its best during the months of November and December. Avoid buying and cooking trout during these two months if at all possible although you can use frozen trout which has been caught at another time of year.

Serves 6

1 x 1.5kg/3lb 5oz trout, scaled and gutted

2 tbsp plain white flour

200g/7oz unsalted butter

3 tbsp olive oil

500g/1lb 2oz shiitake or oyster mushrooms, coarsely chopped

3 tbsp chopped fresh parsley

salt and freshly ground black pepper

2 tbsp very fine dried white breadcrumbs (See Tip)

1 small onion, chopped

1   Preheat the oven to 400F/200C/Gas 6. Coat the fish in flour, then slash diagonally across the back four times on each side. Melt a quarter of the butter in a wide frying pan until foaming. Lay the fish in the butter and cook gently for 6 minutes on each side. Turn off the heat, cover the pan tighty and set aside.

2   Place one tablespoon of butter and the olive oil in a pan, add the mushrooms and cook for 5 minutes or until soft. Stir in the parsley and season to taste. Arrange the mushrooms on the base of an oval ovenproof dish large enough to take the fish. Lay the fish over the mushrooms and pour over the butter in which the fish was cooked. Season to taste and sprinkle with the breadcrumbs. Bake for 7 minutes or until the breadcrumbs are golden brown.

3   Meanwhile, melt the remaining butter in a small pan until golden brown, stir in the onion, remove from the heat and leave to stand for 4 minutes. Strain the flavoured butter into a sauce boat and serve with the fish.

Nutrition notes per serving: *618 calories, Protein 50g, Carbohydrate 10g, Fat 42g, Saturated fat 20g, Fibre 1g, Added sugar none, Salt 0.87g.*

TIP

To make fine dried breadcrumbs: first, make fresh white breadcrumbs. Stand a coarse grater in a large bowl. Rub chunks of bread, crusts removed, on the grater to reduce it to breadcrumbs. Or, whizz bread chunks in a food processor. For dried crumbs: bake in a very low oven (or residual heat from cooking) without browning. Reduce to fine crumbs by whizzing in a food processor.
✳ Place the fresh or dried breadcrumbs in a sealed polythene bag and freeze. Defrost at room temperature or use from frozen.

Vegetable Dishes

BAKED CELERY (SEDANI AL FORNO)

This is ideal for a light lunch. Serve with a green salad and crusty bread.

Serves 6

900g/2lb celery, cut into 10cm/4in lengths

salt

1 large onion, chopped

1 slice prosciutto crudo, cut into julienne strips

85g/3oz unsalted butter

½ tsp beef extract

85g/3oz Groviera or Gruyère cheese, grated

1 Preheat the oven to 375F/190C/Gas 5. Boil the celery in salted water for 5 minutes, then drain thoroughly.

2 Fry the onion and prosciutto in half the butter for 5 minutes or until soft. Stir in the celery and beef extract and fry for 8 minutes. Transfer to an ovenproof dish and sprinkle with the cheese. Melt the remaining butter and pour over the celery. Bake for 5 minutes or until the cheese has melted.

Nutrition notes per serving: *192 calories, Protein 6g, Carbohydrate 4g, Fat 17g, Saturated fat 11g, Fibre 2g, Added sugar none, Salt 0.87g.*

Ⓥ **Vegetarian option:** *leave out the prosciutto crudo and replace the beef extract with a vegetarian yeast extract.*

ROASTED PEPPERS (PEPERONI ARROSTO)

Usually part of an antipasto dish, serve with lots of crusty bread to mop up the juices.

Serves 6

6 assorted coloured peppers

salt and freshly ground black pepper

6 tbsp olive oil

3 garlic cloves, chopped

3 tbsp chopped fresh parsley

6 canned anchovy fillets in oil, drained and sliced in half lengthways, to garnish (optional)

1 Blanch the peppers in boiling salted water for 30 seconds. Drain and place separately in food bags. Close the bags loosely and set aside for 5 minutes. Remove peppers, rub off outer skins with a cloth. Halve, then remove seeds.

2 Cut peppers into wide strips and lay on a grill rack. Brush with oil and sprinkle with garlic, parsley, salt and pepper. Grill on one side for 5 minutes or until slightly blackened and piping hot. Garnish with the anchovy fillets, if using. Serve hot or cold with extra olive oil, if liked.

Nutrition notes per serving: *148 calories, Protein 3g, Carbohydrate 8g, Fat 12g, Saturated fat 2g, Fibre 3g, Added sugar none, Salt 0.48g.*

TIP

You can also skin peppers by pushing a fork into the stalk base and holding over a naked flame, such as a lit gas ring, a candle or under the grill. Turn them round until they blacken and blister. Place in a plastic bag and leave to sweat for 10 minutes, then rub off the skin using a cloth or kitchen paper.

PAN-FRIED TURNIPS WITH SUGAR (RAPE ALLO ZUCCHERO)

I particularly like turnips cooked like this, especially when served with pork dishes.

Serves 6

55g/2oz unsalted butter

1.5kg/3lb 5oz turnips, thickly sliced

salt

2 tbsp icing sugar

2 tbsp plain white flour

300ml/½ pint vegetable or Chicken stock (page 62)

1 Melt the butter in a wide, deep frying pan, add the turnips and turn to coat thoroughly in the butter. Season to taste with salt.

2 Mix together the sugar and flour and sprinkle over the turnips to almost completely coat. Stir once or twice, then pour over the stock, bring to the boil and cover loosely. Simmer, stirring frequently, for 10 minutes or until the turnips are cooked through. The end result should be tenderly soft turnips coated in a smooth, glossy sauce.

Nutrition notes per serving: *169 calories, Protein 3g, Carbohydrate 22g, Fat 8g, Saturated fat 5g, Fibre 6g, Added sugar 5g, Salt 0.43g.*

TIP

Parsnips are also delicious cooked this way. But leave out the sugar as they are already sweet.

SPINACH WITH GROVIERA CHEESE AND HAM
(SPINACI CON GROVIERA E PROSCIUTTO)

This works well on its own as a light lunch, perhaps with some bread and a tomato salad.

Serves 6

2kg/4¼lb fresh spinach

115g/4oz unsalted butter

1 small tumbler milk

salt

115g/4oz ham, sliced into strips

115g/4oz Groviera or Gruyère cheese, grated

55g/2oz Parmesan, freshly grated

1 Preheat the oven to 350F/180C/Gas 4. Steam the spinach for a few minutes, until just cooked, then drain, squeeze dry and chop coarsely.

2 Heat half the butter in a deep frying pan, add the spinach and mix together, then add the milk and season to taste with salt.

3 Use the remaining butter to grease an ovenproof dish. Tip the spinach into the dish, sprinkle with the ham and cheese, then cover with Parmesan. Bake for 8 minutes or until the cheese melts, then serve.

Nutrition notes per serving: *381 calories, Protein 22g, Carbohydrate 6g, Fat 30g, Saturated fat 17g, Fibre 7g, Added sugar none, Salt 2.41g.*

RED CABBAGE (CAVOLO ROSSO)

This is a really wonderful dish to serve with pork or game. In Trentino they still call this vegetable Rotkohl, and indeed it does sound more authentic in German. I like it very much with roast pheasant or goose. Speck is a kind of smoked ham from Trentino.

Serves 4

1 large onion, thinly sliced

85g/3oz Speck or smoked prosciutto or smoked streaky bacon

2 tbsp olive oil

55g/2oz butter

1 glass strong red wine

900g/2lb red cabbage, shredded

salt and freshly ground black pepper

1 In a large pan, fry the onion and Speck gently in the olive oil and butter, stirring frequently, until soft. Add the wine and cabbage, stir, season and cover so that the cabbage retains its colour.

2 Cook slowly, stirring occasionally, for 35 minutes or until the cabbage is the texture you like – the longer you leave it cooking, the mushier it will become. Serve hot.

Nutrition notes per serving: *325 calories, Protein 6g, Carbohydrate 12g, Fat 26g, Saturated fat 11g, Fibre 6g, Added sugar none, Salt 1.12g.*

TIP

Dice a crisp, sour apple and add to the cabbage about half-way through cooking time for extra flavour.

CHICK PEAS WITH TOMATOES (CECI AL POMODORO)

This is a very good one-dish light lunch recipe, delicious with a green salad and some cheese. Adding bicarbonate of soda helps dried chick peas to soften and makes them more digestible. You can use canned chick peas that have been drained and rinsed to considerably cut down the cooking time.

Serves 6

500g/1lb 2oz dried chick peas, soaked overnight

½ tsp bicarbonate of soda

1 large onion, finely chopped

1 garlic clove, crushed

5 tbsp olive oil

115g/4oz pancetta or smoked streaky bacon, coarsely chopped (See Tip, page 24)

400g canned tomatoes, seeded and chopped

salt and freshly ground black pepper

1 Drain the chick peas and place in a large pan with 2 litres/3½ pints of water and the bicarbonate of soda. Bring to the boil, cover and simmer gently for 1 hour or until tender.

2 Meanwhile, fry the onion and garlic in the oil for 5 minutes or until soft and golden, then add the pancetta and fry for 10–15 minutes. Stir in the tomatoes and simmer for 20 minutes, stirring frequently, then season to taste.

3 Drain the chick peas and add to the sauce. Heat through thoroughly, adding extra seasoning, if required, then serve. This is equally delicious cold.

Nutrition notes per serving: *459 calories, Protein 22g, Carbohydrate 48g, Fat 21g, Saturated fat 6g, Fibre 10g, Added sugar 1.88g, Salt 1.59g.*

Desserts

RICOTTA PUDDING (DOLCE DI RICOTTA)

Serve with sliced fresh peaches, oranges or poached dried apricots.

Serves 4

400g/14oz very fresh ricotta

55g/2oz icing sugar, sifted

3 egg yolks

4 tbsp dark rum

1 tbsp Marsala wine

200ml/7fl oz whipping cream, whipped until fairly stiff

langues de chat biscuits, to serve

1 Mix together the ricotta, icing sugar and egg yolks until you have a light, smoothly blended mixture. Stir in the rum and the Marsala, then carefully fold in the whipped cream. Pour the mixture into individual bowls or stemmed glasses, chill for 3 hours, then serve with the biscuits.

Nutrition notes per serving: *467 calories, Protein 13g, Carbohydrate 18g, Fat 35g, Saturated fat 13g, Fibre none, Added sugar 14g, Salt 0.32g.*

! Caution: Both these dishes contain raw eggs.

COFFEE AND CHOCOLATE MASCARPONE DESSERT (TIRAMISU)

This popular Italian dessert tastes better made a day in advance.

Serves 4

250g/9oz mascarpone

4 eggs, separated

4 tbsp caster sugar

2 tsp espresso coffee

115g/4oz bitter cooking chocolate, broken into small pieces

8 tbsp weak coffee

6 tbsp rum, brandy, or Tia Maria

20 boudoir biscuits or savoiardi

2 tsp cocoa powder

2 tsp instant coffee powder

1 Whisk the mascarpone until soft. Beat the egg yolks until pale, then whisk them into the cheese. Very gradually add the sugar to the mascarpone mixture, stirring and whisking constantly. Pour in the espresso coffee and mix thoroughly. Beat the egg whites until very stiff, fold into the mascarpone mixture, then gently mix in the chocolate.

2 Mix together the weak coffee and the liqueur. Dip half the biscuits in this mixture one at a time and use to line the base of a bowl. Pour over half the mascarpone mixture. Dip remaining biscuits in the liquid and use to cover the mascarpone layer. Pour over the remaining mascarpone mixture. Bang the dish down lightly to settle the layers. Mix together the cocoa and coffee powders and sift over the dessert. Chill for at least 3 hours, preferably overnight.

Nutrition notes per serving: *741 calories, Protein 12g, Carbohydrate 53g, Fat 49g, Saturated fat 28g, Fibre 1g, Added sugar 39g, Salt 0.64g.*

TIP

Use good quality coffee and chocolate. You can use almost any liqueur for this dessert. I don't recommend Sambuca, but Amaretto is delicious.

TRENTINO MERINGUE TRIFLE

(SOFFIATO ALLA TRENTINA)

This is one of my great standbys, a simple store-cupboard pudding which everybody loves.

Serves 4–6

250g/9oz boudoir biscuits

rum

700ml/1¼ pints custard

200g/7oz amaretti biscuits or macaroons, crushed

4 egg whites

5 tbsp caster sugar

1 tbsp alchermes or sweet vermouth

1 Preheat the oven to 375F/190C/Gas 5. Soak the biscuits in rum and arrange them on the base of a pretty ovenproof dish. Cover with half the custard. Soak the amaretti biscuits in rum and set aside.

2 Beat the egg whites until stiff, fold in the sugar and the alchermes. Spoon on top of the custard, cover with the remaining custard and sprinkle with the soaked amaretti biscuits. Bake for 20 minutes or until golden, then serve.

Nutrition notes per serving for four: *828 calories, Protein 18g, Carbohydrate 120g, Fat 32g, Saturated fat 12g, Fibre 2g, Added sugar 46g, Salt 1.15g.*

MILANESE CHARLOTTE

(CHARLOTTE ALLA MILANESE)

This is one of my favourite puddings.

Serves 6–8

800g/1¾lb crisp dessert apples, such as Spartan or Cox, peeled, cored and sliced

140g/5oz granulated sugar

2 tsp grated lemon rind

½ glass dry white wine

40g/1½oz butter

1 stale French stick, thinly sliced and crusts removed

140g/5oz sultanas or raisins, soaked in warm water for 15 minutes, drained and dried

2 tbsp pine nuts

1 wine glass dark or white rum

1 Place the apples in a pan with 125g/4½oz of the sugar, the lemon rind, wine and enough water to just cover. Cook on a low to medium heat until the apples are starting to fall apart, transfer to a bowl and cool completely.

2 Preheat the oven to 350F/180C/Gas 4. Blend the butter with the remaining sugar and spread some of it generously around the sides and across the base of a 25cm/10in round Charlotte mould or soufflé dish (not a ring mould).

3 Line the base and sides of the dish completely with the bread slices, reserving enough to cover the top of the pudding. Fill the centre almost to the top with layers of apples, sultanas and pine nuts. Spread reserved bread slices with remaining butter and sugar mixture and use to cover the top. Bake for 1 hour.

4 Turn out on to a plate, pour over rum. Set alight and carry, flaming, to the table.

Nutrition notes per serving for six: *471 calories, Protein 6g, Carbohydrate 78g, Fat 11g, Saturated fat 4g, Fibre 4g, Added sugar 25g, Salt 0.75g.*

TIP

Warm the rum in small pan or metal ladle over a low heat before pouring over the Charlotte and igniting. This is known as flambéing (flaming) and although the actual alcohol is burned off, the flavour remains.

Basic Recipes

BASIC TOMATO SAUCE

(SALSA AL POMODORO)

This is ideal to enrich and enliven all kinds of sauces, soups and stews. It will keep in the fridge for four days and you can use it rather like a stock cube or as sauce in its own right for pasta, risotto or casseroles. You can add flaked tuna fish, pitted chopped olives, mushrooms or anything else that takes your fancy.

Makes enough for 500g/1lb 2oz pasta

3 tbsp olive oil, vegetable oil, butter or margarine

1 carrot, finely chopped

1 onion, finely chopped

1 stick celery, finely chopped

2 tbsp chopped fresh mixed herbs or parsley

400g can tomatoes, drained, seeded and puréed

salt and freshly ground black pepper

1 Heat the oil and fry the carrot, onion, celery and herbs until the onion is soft and transparent. Add the tomatoes and stir thoroughly. Season, then simmer, covered, for 30 minutes.

❄ *Cool quickly, then freeze. Can be frozen for up to 1 month.*

CHICKEN STOCK

Stocks can also be made with beef, fish or vegetables. They are not as fiddly as broth and are generally less rich. Their flavour, however, is very important. This will keep in the fridge for four days.

Makes about 850ml/1½ pints

1 cooked chicken carcase or ½ raw chicken, jointed

2 pinches of salt

1 onion, quartered

1 stick celery, halved

1 carrot, halved

1 Place all the ingredients in a large pan or stockpot with 1.2 litres/ 2 pints of water, stir once and cover. Bring to the boil slowly and simmer for 2 hours. Remove from the heat, cool completely, then strain into a bowl or jug.

❄ *Cool quickly, then freeze. Can be frozen for up to 6 weeks.*

PIZZA DOUGH

It is always best to use fresh yeast for pizza bases if at all possible.

Makes 4 pizzas

400g/14oz plain white strong flour

40ml/1½fl oz water and milk in equal quantitites, mixed together

1 cherry-sized lump fresh yeast or 1½ tsp dried yeast

2 tbsp olive oil

½ tsp salt

1 Place the flour on the table top in a mountain shape. Make a hole in the centre with your fist. Mix the liquid with the yeast until completely dissolved, then pour into the hole. Add the oil and salt, and knead very thoroughly, adding a little flour if it appears too tacky.

2 Knead energetically for about 15 minutes until smooth and elastic and no longer sticky. Place in a bowl, cover with a napkin and place somewhere warm and draught-free to rise for 1 hour.

3 Dust lightly with flour, knock back, then divide into four or leave whole for a large pizza. Flatten out on to an oiled baking sheet. Use your hands, oiled with a little olive oil, to stretch the dough as thinly as possible. It will automatically spring back and shrink, but it is up to you to push and squash it into position.

Other Titles in the *TV Cooks* Series

Michael Barry Cooks Crafty Classics
Ken Hom Cooks Chinese
Madhur Jaffrey Cooks Curries

INDEX